KEN ROBBINS

Earth

THE ELEMENTS

HENRY HOLT AND COMPANY · NEW YORK

Henry Holt and Company, Inc.
Publishers since 1866
115 West 18th Street
New York, New York 10011

Henry Holt is a registered
trademark of Henry Holt and Company, Inc.

Published in Canada by Fitzhenry & Whiteside Ltd.,
195 Allstate Parkway, Markham, Ontario L3R 4T8.

Library of Congress Cataloging-in-Publication Data
Robbins, Ken. Earth : the elements / Ken Robbins.
1. Earth—Juvenile literature.   2. Earth sciences—
Juvenile literature.   [1. Earth.]   I. Title.
QB631.4.R63   1994   550—dc20   94-28019

ISBN 0-8050-2294-5

First Edition—1995

Printed in the United States of America
on acid-free paper. ∞

1   3   5   7   9   10   8   6   4   2

The photographs for this book are hand colored
with water-based dyes.

This book is for Kate and Eliza

STONE FENCE, WORTHINGTON, MASSACHUSETTS

The name of our planet and the land that we stand on; rocks and dirt and mud and sand; the soil in which our crops are grown; the land we own; the bricks and steel with which we build; farms and parks and baseball fields; backyards, front yards, and real-estate deals; the gold and gems that measure wealth; everything that's hard and solid, substantial and dense, from Mount Rushmore to an old stone fence; forests; grasslands; mountains and plains; concrete structures like buildings and roads; the banks of rivers and the shores of seas: these are only a hint of all the things that earth means.

THE EARTH FROM SPACE

The earth is first of all a lonely planet set in space. It's the only one we know of where conditions were exactly right for the slow development of life. The earth looks vast and flat from where we stand, but seen from space, it's a small round ball and doesn't look so very vast at all.

PU'O O'O VOLCANO, KILAUEA, HAWAII

<u>V O L C A N O</u>

We live on the earth's solid, outer crust, where it's cool enough for us to exist. The crust on average is twenty miles thick. Below the crust is the mantle, a very hot region of stuff called magma—squooshy, semimolten matter on which the crust floats. Below that is the core of the earth. At a temperature of nine thousand degrees everybody knows that it's very hot, but no one is sure if it's solid or not.

Volcanoes erupt when magma pushes up through a weak spot in the earth's crust. As the magma rises it begins to expand, and as it nears the surface it explodes, filling the sky with an enormous load of dust and gas and flaming ash. Once the magma hits the air it's known as lava, and it begins to flow, a fountain of fire, a river of flame, leveling everything in its way.

When the eruption is over and that dust and ash and lava settle down, it all cools and hardens and forms a mound. The mound is often in the shape of a cone, with a hole called a crater or vent that runs down the center. Over the centuries that's the way some of the world's greatest mountains were made.

VOLCANO

EARTHQUAKE DAMAGE NEAR LOS GATOS, CALIFORNIA

E A R T H Q U A K E

The crust of the earth—dry land as well as the ocean floor—is divided into gigantic plates, which float and shift around on the mantle. Each plate moves perhaps two inches in the course of a year. In ten million years, so the experts say, Los Angeles may be sitting in San Francisco Bay.

It often happens that plates collide, or one will brush another's side. That produces stresses underground, and an earthquake is the earth's way of easing the tension and settling back down. Sometimes a quake is just a tiny tremor, rattling glasses and cracking plaster, but sometimes it's a great disaster, destroying things and taking lives.

EARTHQUAKE

WHITEFACE MOUNTAIN NEAR WILMINGTON, NEW YORK

M O U N T A I N S

OLYMPIA MOUNTAINS NEAR PORT ANGELES, WASHINGTON

When the floating plates of the earth collide head-on, the crust of the earth will buckle and slide, break up and rise, fold over and thrust. This process over millions of years will change an entirely level plain into a high and jagged mountain range. The Rocky Mountains and the Adirondacks were both formed in exactly that way. The Rockies are still high and jagged today. The Adirondack Mountains, being much older and so much more eroded, are rounded and smoother, not nearly as high or as rugged and steep, and the valleys between them aren't nearly as deep.

MOUNTAINS

DEVIL'S TOWER, SOUTH DAKOTA

IGNEOUS ROCK

LAVA FIELD, McKENZIE PASS, OREGON

There are basically three kinds of rock. Igneous rock was magma once, part of the mantle that's under the crust. Igneous means fiery, which refers to the fact that the rock was so hot once that it melted entirely. When some of that magma intrudes on the crust, it pushes up from below, then begins to cool down. Some cools slowly while it's still underground and turns into igneous rock that's hard and dense. Some becomes lava and flows down the sides of active volcanoes. Compared with the other kind, it's porous and light.

Sometimes magma pushes up but not all the way out of a volcanic cone, filling the volcano's crater like a plug in a spout, and when it cools off, it is very hard rock. In a few million years erosion removes the soft ash and lava that had made up the cone, leaving that dense plug of rock to stand all alone.

IGNEOUS ROCK

SEDIMENTARY ROCK, WATKINS GLEN, NEW YORK

S E D I M E N T A R Y   R O C K

SEDIMENTARY ROCK AND TREES, WATKINS GLEN, NEW YORK

Water from rains or melting snow collects in streams and rivers, which eventually flow to the sea. Tiny particles of rock and sand get carried along by that water and they settle down to the ocean floor, where they're called sediment. This grainy stuff keeps piling up layer after layer, for ages and ages, until under the pressure of its own weight, the bottom layers turn to stone. Some of this rock stays under the sea, but sometimes the sea dries up and recedes. Sometimes, because of the movements of the tectonic plates, the ocean floor buckles and is lifted up and sedimentary rock from the bottom of the sea winds up where you'd least expect it to be, on the side of a mountain or the top of a hill.

SEDIMENTARY ROCK

MARBLE SCULPTURE, SOUTHAMPTON, NEW YORK

Heat and pressure can change many things, not just the way those things look or feel but their very structure, how they're made. Metamorphic rock has been changed in that way. Pressure from the weight of the rocks on top of it and heat from magma that's glowing hot can turn a sedimentary rock like limestone, which is soft and rough, into marble, which is very different stuff. Marble has a smooth and beautiful look. When it's shaped and polished, it looks so good that sculptors often use it to make their art.

METAMORPHIC ROCK

FOSSIL FISH FOUND NEAR PROVO, UTAH

In ancient seas when a fish or some other creature died, it sank to the bottom, where it would lie until its flesh rotted away. If in the meantime the sediment kept piling on, covering the skeleton of this once-living thing, then millions of years later when the sand turned into stone, the rock would contain an impression of the fish's bones. That kind of impression, called a fossil, makes it possible for scientists to know what living things were like a very long time ago.

FOSSILS

SAND DUNES, FLORENCE, OREGON

S A N D   A N D   S O I L

EXPOSED SOIL NEAR NASHVILLE, TENNESSEE

Rocks break up when they rub together; they fracture and fragment when exposed to the weather. Over millions of years, they're ground down into tiny particles of sand.

All by itself, of course, sand is just sand. Nothing can grow in it unless it contains a substantial amount of organic matter. Organic is a word we use to describe anything that was once part of something alive: dead leaves, dead wood, pine cones, a lost toenail, dead flesh and bones, the by-products of living things, like manure and spit and fallen hair. When all this organic matter breaks down and combines with the ground-up sand, that's how soil is made. Soil sits on top of the land, a thin layer, a narrow band of soft and fertile earth.

SAND AND SOIL

FARMLAND NEAR SPARTA, WISCONSIN

FOOD FROM THE EARTH

STILL LIFE WITH FRUIT

The wonder of the earth, its greatest gift, is that it protects that seed and hoards the rain, nurturing the growth that begins the chain of food. The farmer plows the soil and sows the seed that will become the food we need. In the same way, the worm eats the leaf and the bird eats the worm. The bird is eaten by a fox in turn. Eventually the fox will die and its body decay, but the materials from which it's made enrich the soil all over again—part of the endless cycle of living, everything taking and everything giving.

FOOD FROM THE EARTH

DUST STORM AND AUTOMOBILE NEAR RITZVILLE, WASHINGTON

DUST STORM

DUST STORM AND HIGHWAY NEAR RITZVILLE, WASHINGTON

The roots of plants preserve the ground by holding down the loose soil. Without those roots the rain would wash the soil away. But the absence of rain can do even more harm to any field or any farm, because drought can dry out the soil so badly that when the wind picks up and really blows, the soil is picked up too, and goes.

DUST STORM

GRAND CANYON, NORTH RIM, ARIZONA

E R O S I O N

BUTTES AND MESAS, FARMINGTON, NEW MEXICO

The faster water flows, the more power it has to wash away the things it touches as it passes. A little water running for a fairly short while can gouge a little gully in a pile of mud. But the Colorado River, over millions of years, has dug the Grand Canyon, a mile deep and ten wide.

EROSION

SEA STACKS, HECETA BEACH, OREGON

S E A   S T A C K S

SEA STACK NEAR NEWPORT, OREGON

At the edge of the land there's a struggle that goes on constantly between the resistance of the earth and the persistence of the sea. Where the waves pound away at a sea-facing cliff, the rocks get battered and weakened. The softer rocks break down and wash away; the harder parts hold fast and stay. Eventually the sea surrounds the parts that resist the attack of the pounding surf. The resulting formations are called sea stacks, just one more of the many ways that the earth is eroded by wind or wave.

SEA STACKS

HIGHWAY CONSTRUCTION NEAR LEXINGTON, KENTUCKY

EARTH MOVING

CLEAR-CUT FOREST NEAR OLYMPIA, WASHINGTON

Nature is not the only force affecting the earth today. The force of human
nature also comes into play. If the world isn't just as we want it to be, we're
tempted to push it around as we please, scraping the earth and scarring its skin,
gouging out landfills and filling them in, stripping the forests and knocking down
trees, covering the earth with sidewalks and streets. There are too many people in
too little space, and we're in danger of poisoning the earth with our wastes.

EARTH MOVING

PINE FOREST, WOODSTOCK, NEW YORK

The kind of vegetation you find in a place (or the lack of it, in certain cases) defines the nature of the space. Woodlands, of course, are covered by trees, with their roots in the earth, with their branches and leaves and their tops in the sky. Trees make shelter from sunlight and a break from the wind. We take oxygen from the air, but trees put it back in. And for the thousands of animals that live in the woods, trees are kind of like neighborhoods, providing a home for squirrels and birds, arboreal ticks, tree frogs, tree snakes, possums and monkeys, and thousands of other creatures besides.

WOODLANDS

TALLGRASS PRAIRIE, RED CLOUD, NEBRASKA

Grasslands, for the most part, are wide-open spaces. They're not like your lawn; they're natural places where all kinds of grasses naturally grow. Prairies are grasslands, and so are savannas, meadows and leas, the steppes, and the pampas. Once millions of bison roamed the Great Plains. Now only a tiny fraction of the number remains, and the grasslands themselves have been whittled down—most plowed up for farmland, some turned into towns.

GRASSLANDS

DESERT ARROYO NEAR TRUCHAS, NEW MEXICO

T H E   D E S E R T

DESERT, MONUMENT VALLEY, ARIZONA

The desert is a land without much water, and with so little water not much life can take hold. No trees, few grasses—an occasional cactus and a few hardy bushes are all the plant life you're likely to see. It's a strange and beautiful place, where the landscape is naked and the earth is exposed to the sun and the cold. The rocks in the desert break down into sand from expanding and shrinking as temperatures swing. They're also eroded by the force of the wind. But with nothing organic to add to the mixture, the sand doesn't make a very good soil, so the land remains harsh and more or less barren, and only the hardiest life-forms endure.

THE DESERT

WETLANDS, EAST HAMPTON, NEW YORK

WETLANDS

BAYMEN AND WETLANDS, EAST HAMPTON, NEW YORK

Wetlands are marshes and bogs and moist, swampy places, rich fertile spaces between open water and truly dry ground. Sand and silt and sediment and mud carried by the tidal flood or swept along by roiling rivers get trapped in spaces between the roots and stalks of plants, and as a result, they build up the land. These kinds of sites are breeding grounds for frogs and snakes, fish and fowl of many types, insects, mollusks, shrimps and more. Wetlands are delicate, their fragile ecology easily ruined, but because of the richness of the life that they shelter, wetlands are places we need to protect.

WETLANDS

POTTER'S HANDS AND CLAY

C L A Y

POTTER AND CLAY POT

Clay is nothing but mud of a particular kind, and mud is just rock that's been ground up unusually fine. Clay is easy to mold, and in any shape because it's soft when it's moist, but gets hard when it's heated in an oven and baked. That makes it particularly practical stuff. Among the very first things that humans ever made are useful objects of clay: jars for storage and pots and plates and tiles and bricks and pitchers and bowls. Clay pots have been found that are ten thousand years old.

C L A Y

PUMPING OIL NEAR FARGO, NORTH DAKOTA

COAL AND OIL

Many millions of years ago, billions of tiny creatures died and settled to the bottom of ancient seas, and more piled up on top of these. Eventually sand and silt pressed down on them and began to squeeze. When the sand and silt were turned to rock, the creatures were trapped between the layers. Hundreds of feet beneath the soil, those tiny creatures turned into oil.

In ancient, swampy forests great masses of vegetation grew, and over millions of years they too were buried. They too were compressed and subjected to heat. When the transformation was complete and whole, the dead plants had been changed into coal.

Wherever coal or oil can be found, someone wants to dig or pump it out of the ground. The whole world wants these fossil fuels, to heat their homes and power their tools and run their buses, trucks, and cars. But there's a limited amount of coal and oil, and limited amounts only go so far before they run out. A minute or two is all it takes to burn a lump of coal it took millions of years to make.

OPEN PIT COPPER MINE, BINGHAM CANYON, UTAH

MINES

DIESEL ELECTRIC SHOVEL, BINGHAM CANYON, UTAH

Below the earth are many things we've come to need. Metals, coal, and oil spring to mind, but there are thousands of useful ores and minerals that we get from mines—some are easy, some are hard to find. And there are other things that out of greed we convince ourselves that we really need. Gold and diamonds, once they're dug up from the ground, are among the things we value most. So we sink our mines into the earth and rip things up, blasting and scraping to find some more of whatever it is that we're looking for.

MINES

ANASAZI CAVE DWELLING, NEW MEXICO

D W E L L I N G S

PUEBLO BUILDING, NEAR SANTA FE, NEW MEXICO

Many creatures live in the earth: worms, ants, moles, prairie dogs and mice and other animals, all live in holes. Snakes live in pits and bears in dens. Ancient people lived in caves: some caves were simply found and some were made by gouging them out of soft, volcanic rock. Some people live in houses made of wood, which isn't always considered part of the earth (though when you think about it, it should be). But nearly every building or home contains at least some mud or brick, metal or stone, concrete or plaster—all these materials come from the ground.

DWELLINGS

POND AND CEMETERY, EAST HAMPTON, NEW YORK

RITUAL

HOPEWELL INDIAN BURIAL MOUND, CHILLICOTHE, OHIO

Ashes to ashes and dust to dust. Wood decays and iron rusts. Everything changes because everything must. People say man is a hundred pounds of clay, and while that's not exactly true, as a metaphor it's close enough: 10 percent of us is mineral stuff and the rest is water that evaporates away. What happens when we die is hard to say, but it's interesting to note, for what it's worth, that most cultures return their dead to the earth.

RITUAL

For invaluable help, encouragement, and patience, thanks are due to
(among many others), Dava Sobel, Irene Tully, Larry McCormick, Faith Hamlin,
Brenda Bowen, Christy Ottaviano, and as always, Maria.

All hand-coloring by Ken Robbins
All photographs by Ken Robbins except as noted below:
The earth from space on page 7 from NASA
Volcano photograph on page 8 by Greg Vaughn
Earthquake photo on page 10 by Mark Downey
The bust of Julius Caesar on page 18 is from the Village Collection
of the Parrish Art Museum, Southampton, New York.
It was photographed with its kind permission.